for

the many

not

the few

volume 26

ISBN: 9798362428655

All Rights Reserved
Named authors and contributors ©2022
Art work front cover Meek ©2022

The authors of this work have asserted their moral rights.

An Inherit The Earth Publication ©2022
In conjunction with Amazon.

Edited by CT Meek
First published 2022

Other Volumes -
For The Many Not The Few Volume 1
ISBN: 9781719926010
For The Many Not The Few Volume 2
ISBN: 9781728809663
For The Many Not The Few Volume 3
ISBN: 9781730813436
For The Many Not The Few Volume 4
ISBN: 9781790289806
For The Many Not The Few Volume 5
ISBN: 9781793911438
For The Many Not The Few Volume 6
ISBN: 9781797777740
For The Many Not The Few Volume 7
ISBN: 9781092566001
For The Many Not The Few Volume 8
ISBN: 9781077465053
For The Many Not The Few Volume 9
ISBN: 9781688331341
For The Many Not The Few Volume 10
ISBN: 9781697057454
For The Many Not The Few Volume 11
ISBN: 9781709406850
For The Many Not The Few Volume 12
ISBN: 9781677498208
For The Many Not The Few Volume 13
ISBN: 9798618382052
For The Many Not The Few Volume 14
ISBN: 9798646549557
For The Many Not The Few Volume 15
ISBN: 9798664339031
For The Many Not The Few Volume 16
ISBN: 9798692012333
For The Many Not The Few Volume 17
ISBN: 9798700447607
For The Many Not The Few Volume 18
ISBN: 9798743558834
For The Many Not The Few Volume 19
ISBN: 9798532155923
For The Many Not The Few Volume 20
ISBN: 9798752349836
For The Many Not The Few Volume 21
ISBN: 9798779858649

For The Many Not The Few Volume 22
ISBN: 9798418065148
For The Many Not The Few Volume 23
ISBN: 9798808241787
For The Many Not The Few Volume 24
ISBN: 9798836629946
For The Many Not The Few Volume 25
ISBN: 9798849721484

Foreword -

I've always had a love of words, even the ones I don't understand. I feel truly blessed to share these volumes with all of you who continually support and subscribe to what we're doing. Granted, it is incremental to universal poverty, but I personally know how much we influence other people's lives.
Thank you, thank you, thank you.

Meek
November
2022

Authors
Lawrence Reed
Stephen Scott
Meek
Alexander Joe Walsh
Susan Broadfoot
Bobbie O'neill
Andy Greenhouse
Wendy Webb
Annie Foy
Michelle Carr
David Norris-Kay
Seamus Mcleod
George Colkitto
Janette Fenton
George Bakolas
Jon Bickley
Giancarlo Moruzzi
Mark Ingram
Niamh Mahon

Contents -
Allotment
After Our Barras Stoat
Meet The Artist
Canon
A Library Of Horses
Safe Territory
When It Comes To Drugs
The Pale Moonlight
Memento Mori
If The Rain Comes
Far From Gone
Of Poppies
Plough
A Moment Of Stillness
Be Nice To Your Puppy
Walkies
Whisper At The Hearth
Season And The Lunar Cycle
Bugling Winter
Five Shorts
Betrayal (Half Light)
Disputin' The Future
Short, Haiku & Two Cinquain
We Are Family
Beggars' Feast
Birth
Christmas
Distance
Venice
Villanelle For A Dove
The Night I Met My Husband
Blue Flower On Innellan Beach

Rozy's Garden
III Hærvest
Excerpt 1 from the epic poem The Barricade
Excerpt 2 from the epic poem The Barricade
A Slug in the Milk
Despicable Beings
Vampires
The Big Thing Thit's Iverywhere
Frida Kahlo
The Place Of Correction
What I Notice Most!
Slava Ukraini!
Who Am I deluding?
When Autumn Leaves Fall
I Missed The Sun Today
Spider On The Wire
Should We Let The Treasures Sleep?
From The Pulpit
Big Fish/Little Fish
She Looks Up
That Smile
Age
The First Time
Marie Musters Me Her Fragile Delicate Dress
Profile
Forest
Anticipation
Night
New Direction
Ghosts
Needs And Wants
Fortune And Fame
Look At Me
Shitsville UK

November 2022
The Fire Of Oblivion
PANK's Not Dead
Turkey
Jack Kerouac
Anna Karenina
"KLEOS"

Allotment.

Opposite my cottage is a small allotment

Almost a beauty spot

One well-appointed plot near the bottom

is tended by an old liver-spotted man

cloth cap orientated into the hot sun

robotically hoeing

cracking the clods

    of clotted clay

But no seeds are ever sown

The bare strip of sepia sod begs for life

There's a squat rotting brick-red shed

    and a white plastic chair

A conical pile of motely stones in one corner

like a contemplative zen garden

and an old green water bottle

    never employed in this botanic void

An empty terracotta flowerpot stands
        like an afterthought

It's an intricate mystery
        a Gordian knot

It's not polite to ask him why he tends the plot
with all purpose seemingly forgot

but in frustration once I gave it a shot and asked
        "what have you got to grow this year?"

He shrugged and shook his head
        then said "dear oh dear oh dear"

Lawrence Reed.

After Our Barras Stoat.

Nice wee early morning stoat around the Barras with The Greek. Used to be around here loads of times when I went to see Celtic at Paradise. Vast majority of the hostelries are basically known as 'Celtic pubs', the area itself is wholeheartedly 'Glesga'. A few years ago the market was getting a bit shit, most of the stalls where being leased by clothing shop owners, no prices advertised, but the stall holders would quote you a price for an item then quote a different price to someone else for the same item. They would judge you by your appearance and by how affluent you looked. Yet the market is famous for memorabilia, antiques, bric-a-brac et al. Definitely the place to go for your unusual items, a place where you could get £50 cash at a cost of £40, you could get whatever you were after at the Barras. So it was refreshing to feel that old vibe again today, feels like it's turning back to the Barras of old. Lots of hand-made items, the old CD/vinyl stalls are still there, and my favourite stalls, the ones with all the old junk/toys/ornaments are still going strong. A lot of familiar stall holders are still kicking around which is great. One of the stalls I dropped by was ran by a friend's daughter, the lovely Laura. Laura sells crystals and jewellery, lots of healing and spiritual stones (picked up a wee gift for Emily, as I might be on the razzle later 😜) and incense. A lovely positive young lassie, if you are ever around pop by and say hello. After our Barras stoat, our main objective was to visit Blitzkrieg, Tony Gaughan's amazing record shop on the London Road, as I had been singing its praises to The Greek after my last visit. Tony was attending a record fayre so wasn't around, but the lovely Stephanie was at the helm. A cracking shop that is a veritable museum of music, CDs, posters, guitars, clothing. So a productive and enjoyable morning was had. I'm off to The Greeks mansion now to sink a few tins and watch the football. Hope you all have a relaxing and fun weekend. Take care, be kind, stay free ☺🖤✌ .

Stephen Scott.

Meet The Artist.

Had a 'Meet the Artist' evening in Front Room Gallery Helensburgh last night. The seaside town was being lashed with wind and rain and was basically deemed a ghost town, crazy weather. Still, the lure of some prosecco and art proved too strong a magnet for some welcome brave souls. Many thanks to all who came along, some very interesting folk indeed. Have to mention Gary and Iona, a lovely young couple who had just arrived in town after leaving their home in Bristol that morning, on a visit to Iona's parents in the burgh. I enticed them both into the gallery to escape the weather and enjoy the fine wine. During our conversation, Gary mentioned that he had 'sailed' the Atlantic 7 times, had sailed the coast of Scotland, had sailed the Caribbean, had sailed the Norwegian fjords, and added that Iona had sailed the Atlantic, Pacific, Indian Oceans and was far more travelled on a yacht than he was. And here's me saying 'come in out the rain you'll end up soaking'. Must've been like water off a ducks back to them both, literally. Such a lovely couple, as were all the visitors. Wonderful conversations with each and every one, thank you. Thanks to Gallery assistants Gail and Derek who were great company too. ☺♥

Stephen Scott.

Canon.

As a general rule, trembling
With lots going on
Creeping Jesus types wearing
Robes and not much else
Forcing the issue of religious poetry
Masked as medical staff usually are
You do know that we're not long out
Of a recent pandemic
And that writing about it was frowned upon?
Straight
Into a colder vacuum
While monitoring yet another
Claim of the second coming
Wishful thinking if you ask me
When urges are prevalent
And flesh resembles sundried leather
All of your violated appointments, all of your
Surrogate tenets count for nothing here
Among the fractured sperm count
Sacred books considered sacred languish
In a library of horses
(More of which later!)
Similar sounding words plucked from obscurity
You hardly know their meanings
Or the context in which they can be used

Not by fair play

Or equal opportunity

Nor by the criterion of which

Someone is judged

Ignored rank and file, status of the shrew

Take this yardstick for fair play, take this benchmark

As a given

Relocate to a place that is infamous for being

An exemplar of multicultural non-existence

Certainly not upon this sceptic isle

Certainly

Not this unfair formula -

A template for disingenuous absolutes.

Meek.

A Library Of Horses.

We peddled our way through wretched gutters
Shopfront facades offering discount meals
Light rain dampened our cigarettes, the people will come
The people will come

Not until our swimming explodes, and not until
Overcoming moves closer
We know we're being watched, multiple still births
Are unlikely to be introduced

The hunger levels reduce risks, such
Populist drivel is music to financial ears
These poor quarters remain much sought after
Residential areas, impressive upon familiar territory

We star jump our way endlessly without food
Spontaneous love insufficient to nourish us
Perpetually late to the scene, distress signal soon extinguished
Defeated we sugar coat inaccurate information

Uptight about being eliminated, expensive cuts
Made less available, less edible
Mercenary values top parade ground lists
The death of an icon is unveiled

Alongside unemployment the listener strikes again
Funeral hymns for those at spirit level
And all our plans and all our rhyming escapes
Are extracted like rotten teeth

Only when it's mathematically impossible to succeed
Shall we surround arm ourselves with charm offensive
Only then we'll amplify our concerns
And challenge the powers that be

We may be arrested, incarcerated
We may seek asylum in pods and hubs
We may inter our devastated heritage
Revealed to be our last place of refuge.

Meek.

Safe Territory.

You suspend most animation, reality

And aspic crises

Upend equilibrium, ring-fence common etiquette

And the cost of living

You defend corrupt faith, transform friendship

And sit without judgement

Send parasites homeward, update euphemisms

And apprehend bad ideas

You pretend to be circling, under achieving

And grabbing with both hands

Defend your moral rights, delete toxified data

And let impetus diminish.

Meek.

When It Comes To Drugs.

Overhear you sleeping, reciting free speech
Waxing lyrical about mobile phones
Digging deep into darkened sound bites

May have mistaken correct dosage, a design to be still
To weaken omnipresent nuances
Lost in noise, in pure stasis

Body jettisons, televises a third eye party
Small but important syringes
Leave telling tracks

Starved of oxygen, of anti-social drive
Disclosure lives in hope (coated tablets)
It is official the law is illegal

Details make little sense, overdose proves fatal
Adopt a marginalised recovery
Obsess about being within limits.

Meek.

The Pale Moonlight.

(Joker)

Did you dance with the Devil in the pale moonlight?
Did you sweat with greedy passion in the heat of the night?
Did you sleep with an Angel at the foot of your bed?
Did you dance, dance and dance to stop yourself feeling dead?
Did you laugh in the mirror at the face looking back?
Was it yours or another's, did it laugh right back?
Did you scream as you danced and plead to be released?
And feel his embrace tighten as he screamed to be so pleased?

Did you dance with the Devil in the pale moonlight?
To relentless rhythm played to incite and to ignite.
Did you beg to be forgiven as the demon held you tight?
But all your pleadings did were to enflame and to excite.
And as the terror of your lust took grip and hypnotised you,
And your body and your mind were engulfed in the inferno,
Did your Angel abandon you to the seductive throbbing turmoil?
And the Devil laughed again as he claimed your virgin soul.

Did you dance with the devil in the pale moonlight?
Did you pray for your Angel to restore you to the light?
Did you wake in the morning with the remnants of a dream?
That haunted you, and stalked you, and lured you back to sleep.
Where your Angel could not reach you, to soothe you and save you,
And the music and the dance overwhelmed you and possessed you,

And you knew at last the truth that you had always been denied,
Before you danced with the Devil in the pale moonlight!

Alexander Joe Walsh *(July 2020)*

Memento Mori.

"Don't let your halo slip, come to the soiree with me and Ego. Ego is doing well, you'll see. Ego is clean," Gene states quite matter-of-factly. Quite glib, arrogant even. Some would call it conceited. Hubristic. But you had to know Gene to harbour such thoughts and very few do. You had to earn entitlement. And besides, you'd never say it aloud or to Gene's face.

Gene means well. Always does. Always true to every uttered word. Never ventures towards the absurd or untrue. Of course, Gene isn't its real name. It doesn't have a real name: A biological or scientific moniker. Everyone calls it something different. But it does exist; it exists inside all of us. *(Pronoun use has been permitted but unwarranted. Gene is non-binary, genderless and unique.)*

"C'mon, c'mon, you know you wanna, know what I mean," Gene pleads in its best ever Marianne Faithful/ Keith Richards *(post/pre-heroin/mars bar and rug phase)* slurry drawl. I always assume this trait is down to a stroke, or a speech impediment, or maybe attributed to some kind of substance abuse over an indefinite period of time. For all I know it could even be a brain *(malfunction)* programmed alternatively. Wired to its own moon.

I'm just not in the mood. I've hit the skids once again: Buffoon's Dark Canine *(sic)*. I enter anti-social phases where it's just better to shrivel up and become invisible, to stay in. Static enamoured by stasis. Life is shit. It takes the piss. Brutal when it misfires. It assumes. It takes me for granted. Socialising scares me. I have to fight or take flight (*I seldom freeze*), but I'm a pacifist and am carrying a hamstring injury. I can't think of anything worse. Big unknown crowds terrify me. I just don't have anything topical, interesting or relevant to say. And my ears won't listen. I feel like I'm a satellite.

"C'mon you'll enjoy yourself. You know you will, once you get going. What's the worst that can happen? You know these punters. They're on your side, know what I mean?"

Gene just never lets up, states it has experience of what I'm going through. I doubt that, but how would I know? Each individual's ordeal is according to the recipient. Circumstances dictate outcome.

It's only a few days since I drove to the bridge. *The Bridge.* Admittedly I've been harbouring these thoughts for a wee while now. There's nothing glamorous about entertaining Mister Suicide. You don't know if you're a coward or courageous. I'd picked my spot. I actually woke up once in my own absurd vision. It was a brilliantly sunny and warm day and I was mid-way between the East Bridge's span. The exact spot where the Labour Ward woman who'd embezzled her Women's Guild funds and spent all the money on bingo, wine, and cigarettes *(although she didn't smoke or drink)*. A Devout church going woman. You were allowed to say that *(woman)* in those days. She was her local church's treasurer. Had her hand in that till too.

A frumpier parishioner you could ever hope to meet. She'd been in arrears with the rent, electricity, and milk money (*Six weeks milk money due. I know because I was the milk boy*). Her five kids never had playpiece or dinner money, but always had brown sauce sandwiches (*First time I'd heard of brown sauce*) and sometimes pickled onion crisps. She jumped from *The Bridge* just before the school summer holidays. But I digress.

"C'mon, what's stopping you?" Marianne/Keith aka Gene asks.

"I just don't fancy it. I get anxious just thinking about it. I get stressed. People get too close."

"Ach, you don't know what you'll be missing, know what I mean? You were born for this. You overthink things, that's your trouble," Gene intones.

"Yeah, I guess I do. My psychiatrist says it's all to do with my fucked up origins, and the lack of affection and encouragement given. I guess lugging around all this baggage has taken its toll, eh?"

Gene then with words of wisdom bleats, "It's a good kick up the arse that you need. That's the best medicine. That's how it was and how it should be. Never done me any harm. Fuck cognitive therapy."

You know, Gene's within limits not wrong, closer than far away from the truth. Gene is just a few weeks shy of being clean a calendar year. Just thirty five days or so. A breath away from relapse, from falling into dangerous territory again. A deal away from circling with the vultures. I hope I'm wrong. See, I take folk at face value. I see the good in 'em. I'm always the last to know when I'm being played. Is that an appealing trait?

Gene has gone AWOL, abandoned ship, evacuated the building, quit the scene, taken leave of its senses, withdrawn from sobriety, become empty of a space, exited, packed its bags, pulled out, gone away, withdrawn, taken off, skedaddled, relinquished possession, moved out, departed from and fucked off without a word. This is all going through my head as I stand here on the bridge, all boding badly for a positive outcome. As if any of this is important, these muddled euphemisms, these concepts, these assumptions. As if any of it matters. I wonder what the Labour Ward woman was thinking when she stepped off. Did she consider her children? Must've be hellish reaching that crucial point. Taking that leap just beyond it. No turning back.

And now it's my turn. There's no queue, no orderly line. It's an almost perfect day. It is my turn isn't it? Had I stored the Labour Ward woman's story away all these years for some subconscious future alibi? Had I superimposed myself onto and into her tragic narrative?

Mummy lets go of my hand and daddy gives me a gentle nudge, siblings baulk, and lover, you relinquish our hold and avert your gaze. You stole my heart the very first time I set eyes on you. I can't think about you too much now. Everything is condensed, suppressed.

I think I can fly. Life has pummelled me, got the better of me. My lust for it has lost its potency. I think I can fly. I do, I really do. I believe I can sprout wings and take flight. But they say that you're dead before you hit the water, that it's the fall that kills you. It's really the fall that kills you. I think I can hear the Holy Spirit whispering, or maybe it's the rushing air whistling as I descend. I am flying, I am. Alarm bells are ringing. A siren is calling, wailing.

And then I think of you.

You loom large into view like the placid ocean.

This is the last thought I'll have.

Meek.

If The Rain Comes.

If you don't like the weather then change it.

Well, we did it before.

We need to show this planet some love, then show it some more.

But what if it's too late?

Don't we have enough on our plate?

But we could at least try and I'll tell you why:

If the rain comes

The snow falls

And the wind blows

Then the sun will shine

And we will survive

We will survive

We are losing our seasons

They're all forming into one

And we are the reason

Just look at what we have done

Do you hear what I'm saying?

Yes, I'm talking to you

You tell me you've been praying

But there's so much more we could do

If the rain comes
The snow falls
And the wind blows
Then the sun will shine
And we will survive
We will survive

It's a race against time
And we're cutting it fine
If we really want to play our part
We better hurry up and make a start

If the rain comes
The snow falls
And the wind blows
Then the sun will shine
And we will survive
We will survive
We will survive.

Susan Broadfoot.

Far From Gone.

We have always questioned what happens when someone dies
Do they simply turn to dust or go somewhere in the skies?
But there's something I do know
It's what I truly believe
That they remain with us
They never really leave

Far from gone
But still with us by our side
They are far from gone
As sure as the changing tide

It's never easy when times are bad
Your heart is breaking
You feel angry and sad

But you need to remember it wasn't always this way
Re-live all the good times as you think of them today

Far from gone
But here with us by our side
They are far from gone
As sure as the tide

Hearing a whisper in the wind
A gentle touch while you sleep
All the memories you share
Are still with you to keep
Forever . . . Forever

They are far from gone
They will always, always be near . . .

Susan Broadfoot.

Of Poppies.
There
                    wild poppies grow
along the roadside
                      swaying slow
in gentle breezes
                          as I pass

Lift their reds
                    a mile of smiles
to see the verge
                      burst with life
how small
                      these flowers

How deep
                          they burn
like embers
                        in the heart
so quickly gone
                        their trace

That faint mark
                    once so bright
ashes of a flame
                    made dreams
which flared
                      and danced.

George Colkitto
(September 2022)

Plough.

Ground turned deep
So often has he crossed this field
Plough locked in the furrow

He does not step over or round
Soft ground rock or dung
His course was set before knowledge
And now is fixed by his labours

He follows his steady team
Broad-backed horses pull to his voice
Take their route out and back
Blinkered steady uncomplaining
Head down he plods on.

George Colkitto.

A Moment Of Stillness.

(Found and lost on the beach at Seahouses)
Winds drift these dunes
Grasses bind   struggle   to defeat
Storm   gale   scuff of many feet
Beyond duck-boards and picnic debris
Areas cordoned to prevent erosion
Beyond children playing cricket
Men building castles   digging moats
Beyond sight of houses and road
There is transience
Where sea   sand   sky   fall as one
Each step quickly drowned
Each breath lost in blue
Yesterdays float in the wind
Tomorrows threaten the horizon

George Colkitto.

Be Nice To Your Puppy.

Be nice to your puppy
she wants to only play
be nice to your puppy
every day
be nice to your puppy
she only wants to be kind
be nice to your puppy
she wants a surprise
be nice to your puppy
she can't control it
be nice to your puppy
she only wants a hug
be nice to your puppy
she only wants to have fun
be nice to your puppy
she wants to only grow up
be nice to your puppy
even if she wakes you up
at night

Bobbie O'neill.
(Aged 8 ¼)

Walkies.

I'm led through streets

and darkened alleys

where odours permeate

the chilly evening air

I stop, here

beside an interesting lamp post

or occasionally there,

next to one of natures

magnificent arboreal loos

sometimes we meet

a familiar face

and suitable greets

are exchanged and extrication

from entanglement ensues

then we continue

in the fervent hope

we can complete our stroll

without further commotion

but across the road

we see the black and white

loud-mouthed bitch

that nobody likes

and we avoid her

like the plague

I exchange glances

with the one she leads

and we head off

in opposite directions

clutching our bags of poo.

Andy Greenhouse.

Whisper At The Hearth. *(2010)*

Clutching mental crevices,

screaming in silence.

Whispering interludes,

wrapping conglomerations.

Casually stepping across

the intangible.

Grasping recognition,

words weep in the cement mixer

and set.

Bustling in byways,

insinuating publicity;

pausing for recognition.

Demanding deserts in bloom,

parched beside the oasis.

Words - futile, unconscious,

skulking in bone channels;

confined to whispers at another's hearth,

screeching in hollow silence.

Wendy Webb.

Season And The Lunar Cycle.

They used to think the sun revolved
around a static earth;
the land was flat and, domed above,
all planets hung in space.

In gravity we orbit,
calendars counting seasons,
and for a Leap Year's extra day
we reason why the earth rotates
- calculate a year, or so -
day and night's kaleidoscope.

Bright moon keeps pace and orbits earth,
racing with the sea,
as sailors mark charts of their route
from lunar months and, every day,
two tides turn routinely.

Records of Latitude, Longitude,
date morning's cruising Time Lines.
Magnetic fields, volcanoes,
Global Warming's unpredictable weather.

The sun, always expected,
gives light and warmth and life.

I'm glad the earth's not static
and, though it shows its age,
I would not wish it round and flat –
we need revolving space.

Wendy Webb.

Bugling Winter.

As soon as the clocks were turned back,
a sad and tacky damp crawled in,
drifting skin-thin with wretched leaves
and heaps of worm-casts on the lawn,
now worn down dank as mud's rich slime.

Dark encroached its final traces;
afternoon's sad light shivering,
chill winter's clawing nails stretched out
too soon to say goodbye, to fall:
engorging embers, leaves to ash.

Yet summer reared its glorious fight
and kicked the air of freezing dawn,
to flush a lasting colour's mount
upon the winter's saddle, sound
the final hunts of redcoats, hounds.

White trousers muddied, beating rain
and flowers bushed while in full bloom.
Yet, beautiful with damp perfume,
the rose of England's halcyon days
all gone to monochrome winter.

Wendy Webb.

Five Shorts.

The One Show is great before eight,
serves current affairs on a plate.
Tuck in and see why it's tasty and free
when our hosts serve fine morsels in plenty.

Dear One Show, please help, a brass knocker
confused our poor postmen in Norwich.
So rural their rounds, it delayed them from sorting
our mail... for they thought it a bomb.

Dear Pam, this Poem is Waiting
to court you and spit out the pips.
A fig is too modest, sweet cherries are dating,
to drip down your luscious red lips.

Amused, the foetal figure multiplied
confused by fantasies, I could not choose.
Resumed the blueprint of a theme reused -
Muse vanished in the metre of remorse.

I looked up rhymes cooked in this book,
since I yearned for my poem to win.
Quick-thinking vicar chanted sin,
now my 'Nun's Tale's' stuck without fuck.

Betrayal. (Half Light)

Betrayal dies into a tipping hat
that's upturned in a subway pavement's beg
of grimacing as stars of sparking teeth
that lie beneath the rags of hope or death.
The half-moon scoops its wages at the dregs
of cities swept unclean and filled with hope
of coppers, spinning on a single coin,
or pinheads, like a dandelion of angels.

Snake slits of lies that close unshuttered dark
and swallow whole the rat that life's become.
For terror rises with a sickly moon
of street lights raising ghosts on edge of sight.
Gag and regurgitate a spinning tail
of thirty silver pieces in a field,
of twitching, hanging feet where light has dimmed
into an unrepentant thief stretched wide
as heaven on a word of pain, of death.
A gold where Midas' sinews flow to streams,
unstiffened by the Reaper's fearful scythe
upon a sickle moon where wraiths flesh blooms.

Wendy Webb.

Disputin' The Future.

Putin

are you hootin'?

Are you having a bad day?

You give 'em power n armaments,

they post flowers and Olympic play.

Putin

are you mutterin'

all alone in your cold room?

You bang up all the life n joy

like some memorial tomb.

Putin

are you lootin'

productive land n people?

If you need an isolated project,

grow sunflowers, not rocket's steeple.

Putin

you are shootin'

your homeland into history.

A monster megalomaniac;

shame you've left no mystery.

Wendy Webb.

Short, Haiku & Two Cinquain.

Misery day, misery day,
time for soldiers to mourn their dead.
The 9th of May, the 9th of May,
for victory's defeat and dread.

Daffodils dallied
with path beside the river;
seasoned war and peace

It takes
five lines to write
a Cinquain, which simply
means syllable count compressed in
five lines.

A crow
is not a rook,
unless it's in a crowd.
But then, a rook that's on its own's
a crow.

Wendy Webb.

We Are Family.

The slamming woke me up, the whole house shook. My dad's come home. That's the shouting started. Jordan'll sneak through to my bed in a minute.

My mum hates my dad and my dad hates my mum. He's hardly ever here, but when he is, she nags him, and he gets angry and tells her to shut up, and then she gets angry and shouts at him and he shouts back.

Some nights he's not even in the door five minutes before she starts. He brought her a box of chocolates once, but she started anyway. Where's he been since Friday? She's had to beg food off Theresa again. He'd rather give his money to the brewery than feed his weans.

No wonder he stays out, all he gets is earache. And look at the state of her. What did he ever see in her? Fat, ugly cow.

Well he knows where the fucking door is.

One day, my mum was out and he had to watch us. He made Jordan go to the shop for Irn Bru, and Jordan fell coming up the path and he battered his elbow and cut his knee and he got a row off my dad. But when my mum got home, he was still bleeding and she went mental and had to take him to hospital, and they were away for hours, and my dad was watching me but he was really just watching the boxing.

Jordan got three stitches in his knee, and a sling. My dad said how was he supposed to know, he's not a fucking nurse. My mum went, "No, but you're a fucking useless idiot and you might have made the tea."

Jordan and I kept out of the way and he shared his Haribos with me. He got them for being brave.

Jackie's my best pal. Her dad gets drunk sometimes too. One time he fell on the pavement and there was blood all the way to their door. I don't know if he got stitches. Jackie's mum never shouts at him, but he shouts at her and Jackie when he's had a drink. Jackie's mum gives her a piece 'n' crisps and tomato sauce every single day. We never get that.

I've never had stitches, but I got lost once. Well, I didn't know I was lost because I knew where I was, but my mum didn't know and when I got home, she went mental because she'd been hunting for me and she'd reported me, and I'd caused a lot of trouble and a police woman gave me a row as well. If my dad had been there, he'd have gone even more mental.

Jordan says when he grows up he's going to join the police and if anyone starts a fight, he'll put them in the jail. He's only seven.

I'm nine, and I'm going to get a job on a cruise ship, because you get to go hundreds of miles away and you don't even have to come back. You can just go round and round the world for ever. I'll get Jordan a job too, when he's big enough. And my mum can come for her holidays sometimes.

Here he is: he's wet himself. I'll get him clean pyjama bottoms and he can snuggle in beside me. He likes that. So do I.

Sometimes, Jordan and I fall out, but he's my wee brother and I really, really love him.

Annie Foy.

Beggars' Feast.

Swollen sun candescent in cloud
Gathering in the East,
birdsong chorus echoing loud
heralds a beggars' feast.

They drink sweet draughts of open air,
consume the vibrant view:
bright breeze-blown grasses grace their lair,
shining with drenching dew.

Fresh fields of bending barley sway
against far purple hills,
and fruits of nature coaxed from clay
an aching hunger fills..

A perfect praedial repast
for poor man, bird and beast,
who end their bleak bucolic fast
and join the beggars' feast.

David Norris-Kay

Birth.

Dark membranes tremble: slowly slide apart:
Revealing liquid amniotic gloom,
Distant sounds faded by a drumming heart,
Echoing spasms of a fruitful womb:
Dim daylight beckons beyond pulsing pain,
Promising things I cannot understand,
Like flowing rivers, and soft falling rain:
Far-reaching skies over emerald land.
Contractions quaking in my tender ears,
I uncurl quickly, pushed towards the light,
Driven by incipient, feral fears:
Commence the struggle of my mortal fight.

Emerging from Mother's darkness I bring,
Fresh life to the dominion of Spring.

David Norris-Kay.

Christmas.
Beyond the frost-flaked window, snow
transforms a silent tree
and in the fulgent fire-light's glow
flickering shadows flee..

Leaving the rosy light intact
where apparitions form -
inside young minds which interact
with voices in the storm:

They speak of all-enfolding love
where bauble-stars burn bright,
the twinkling galaxies above
cold clouds in velvet night.

The ghost of hope in children's dreams
will drift in thought, and stay,
until the apparition gleams
corporeal as day.

It flies through towns on angel's wings,
sustaining troubled souls.
And while a hushed choir softly sings,
the bell of midnight tolls -

Heralding Yuletide's dawning joys,
where whirling blizzards blow
and stirs the sleep of girls and boys
concealed from falling snow.

The distant church bells echo through
a river's frost fogged haze,
and sweet young voices raise anew
old Christmas hymns of praise.

David Norris-Kay.

(Third prize in the Salopian poetry competition)

Distance.

I left her in the wild wood's thrash,
where wind-rubbed branches percussion
beat a tattoo through our distance.

Passion faltered in the year's grip:
Year upon year, love's force had slipped
down the swirl of adversity -

lost in a swamp-sink of boredom.
Mad-marching legions of routine
had trampled first feelings to dust;

ground us into the barren land
from which we had sprung: Tender green
shoots on a hard city highway.

We are gratefully extinguished
by cold draughts of cruel logic
howling from first fatal passion

seated only in lust: I left
her in the wood's tree-tortured murk,
forlorn, and alone with our child.

David Norris-Kay.

Venice.

I am imprisoned
in the baroque heart
of a sinking city,
where madness drums
through empty hope,
and obsession holds me
like a pinioned moth,
to a sick
inevitable fate.

Motes of darkness
pervade a dusk of domes,
where I hide
in my ectoplasm of shadow,
and wade
through congealing fear -

over the bridge of sighs.

David Norris-Kay.

Villanelle For A Dove.

Beating wings facile in the frosty air,
As snowy skies from far horizons loom,
A white dove rises from its winter lair.

Purity and beauty beyond compare,
Ghosting the borders of a tree-dark gloom,
Beating wings facile in the frosty air.

Symbol of peace that soothes a dark despair,
Where gnarled looped branches tremble and entomb,
A white dove rises from its winter lair.

Faint fading stars briefly blossom and flare,
Light softly shining in my winter room:
Beating wings facile in the frosty air.

Cold gauzy cloud dims a swollen moon's stare,
Mirrored in ice like a petrified bloom:
A white dove rises from its winter lair.

Earth in iron grip, the bent trees leaf-bare,
Roots snow deep, and above their drifted womb -
Beating wings facile in the frosty air;
A white dove rises from its winter lair.

David Norris-Kay.

The Night I Met My Husband.

Michelle Carr.

Blue Flower On Innellan Beach.

Michelle Carr.

Rozy's Garden.

Michelle Carr.

III Hærvest.

i

*
**
***

restored
born before
nights draw in
fresh rites sworn
worn sight set alight
four unmeshed senses
exposed bracken thorns
let me taste your musty air
adorable Autumn splendour
jackdaws store acorns in lawns
the novel spawn of putrefaction
perilous laws of life daily redrawn
special vegetal reek of shaded paths
boys slowly stroke the fallen-leaf floor
corn stubble burns over a war-torn dawn
carrion crow and raven caw over gory relics
fungal zoospores swim across wet porous clay
tusks of truffle-nuzzling boars poke musky roots
sore-billed jackdaws peck at oak-wood back doors

> *like furtive salesmen-whores*
> *like bored murderers nailing floors*

***
**
*

iv

*
**
***

I crush the apricot and mandarin skins
    of fallen leaves, in shapes
        of every denomination
           I have known.
Foliage-fumes and fungus-blotted trunks
    clot the air.
The breeze in the dry leaves
    sounds like dribbling water
A hunter's gunshot echoes,
    scattering crow and chough.
A desperate pneumatic sound
    of startled wood pigeon wings.
The poacher's rough slipknot stills the doe.
This cruel deathblow so lovingly bestowed.

I stroll under the autumnal awnings:
    a Bach-like counterpoint
        of criss-cross boughs
           and branches.
The late-dropping blood beech leaves susurrate
    in a violent sough of the wind.
Needles rain from majestic cedars.

A meadow drainage ditch reflects in its legato flow,
    a storm sky
        growing intensely indigo.
Summer days have been inexorably pruned.

Gyroscopes and dynamos rotate,
        overthrowing tomorrow.

Post-equinoctial sunlight cuts unfamiliar angles
        before a fierce, short squall.

Then a new covenant after the fall.
A double-rainbow sideshow is born.
The lower arc fiercely glows
        over fallow unploughed ground.
But I am besotted
        by the misbegotten, overarching,
                squat sibling of fainter intensity:

        like a shadowy twin jackpot of gold
        like a poor sot's rotten mascot.

iii

*
**
***

sickness
equinox pox
blackbirds bicker
last easy embers flicker
breezes breathe life into trees
leaves gain the gift of mock speech
susurrations and rustles and crackles
rooks perch on a crooked beech branch
rows of Shiva avatars mimic gallows crows
flesh surrenders a leaky reservoir to the far stars
nature is slowly hooked on decay's sharpened barbs
like rusty scrapped cars
like dusty arcane books

***
**
*

iv

*
**
***

fall
retreat
sniffling dogs
rain-stained trunks
dead vacant leaf-veins
colour-softened forebrains
vapoury days of ghosts and Gog
doomed insects try new costumes
badgers trog through dank domains
damp terrain seethes with innate disdain
groggy frogs buried in mouldering remains
strained squashes like acutely swollen wombs
primrose-perfumed frosty fogs suffuse the gloom
worms salute the brutal reign of slower-grinding cogs
stark phallic mushroom-fruit blooms from roots and logs
> *like covered sofas in darkened rooms*
> *like unmarked tombs*

***
**
*

Lawrence Reed.

Excerpt 1 from the epic poem The Barricade.

I stroll past the first cackling coven forming about Mary... Into pint ***five*** now ('man alive!') and carousing full of zip and pep, well-juiced and merry. Saucy Salome (dazzling) and younger Mary M (once a fleeting fling), join the hairier melancholy Mary (posturing). Sat static, as the two 'skin and blisters' systematically approach, to perch on free adjacent barstools for a natter. Symptomatic of this serene sisterhood: sister's sympathy smattered with reproachful sisterly patter, and peppered with blasphemy, by Jove! which ill behoves the coven's sacred clothing.

Mary's 'dressed up to the nine's' in a smart tight costume of periwinkle-blue with silly trims of lily-white. Bless´ed among this group. The peaceful pure pigment of her Marian-blue gauzy cloth protects sacred vessels. Tranquil, light colour of the heavens. Valuable hue, lapis lazuli, azurite.
Heavens above!
I question my frightful, misjudged vermillion jacket lining. Too flaming rakish. Height of bloody allegory. Fatal mistake?

Mary was a Sunday-school teacher at the nearby Baptist hall; before her very scary fall. 'Full immersion' now does what it says on the tin; it's no longer a salvation rite, White doves rarely take flight. What you see is a tenth of what you get (like an iceberg). Mary totters a tight-rope plight. Already tight. She is 'special' all right.

Crossed fish-net stockinged legs. Smutty suspenders, decent bod. Smoky peepers alight. An oddly erotic sight for any dirty old sod. 'Boat race' a bright maroon cast. Glacial heart; might thaw soon, to an all-access pass. Swivelling solitarily and seductively on her voluptuous, ever-ready arse. ('Gordon Bennett'!) Brassy as the Side One painstakingly-polished brass. Gobbling her garnet goblet of Cockburn's Port and flat lemonade full-on fast (class!). Staring cockeyed into the vast, wide, frosted gin-palace looking-glass. Contemplating this ghastly, reversed ghostly-crew on their myriad odysseys;

her last decent ride; and a young girl's life passed over into the weirder Alice-side.

The huge towering etched mirror holds her face, holds our fates, holds this world in place; incorruptible. In order to survive, live with its reflection... or change it.
So endeth the third lesson...

Just to the left there's a sunken gothic arch, framed with pink marble pillars like some relic from more ancient times when it might have housed a Madonna and Child with endlessly burning votive candles: or a prancing Pan breathing lustfully into his flute.

Mary feels half-alive, not bad odds in this dismal dive. Chosen, anointed with Chanel No 5. Tipsy, titty, faintly pretty. It's her assumption life is sodding shitty and claims knowledge of the exact date it will end for her. Strict unscripted secret. Pity. No annunciation.

I'm consumed with affection and arrested by this optical illusion: three snapped, spluttering, chattering Hagettes. Marionettes alluding to alluring grace, framed and contorted in the reflecting silver, splattered under the mighty cut glass mirror-face.

Bleary Mary; clear Salome; dear Mary M.
In that order:
Lost mirth; lost elegance; lost youth.
Tragic, glaucous-grey eyes;
cruel, vaguely challenging been-green eyes;
open, tender blue eyes.
A few sad abortions.
Skin-slack; fat-back; enticing cracks.
No fear; no care; no caution.
Seeing no evil;
      hearing no evil;

swearing in biblical proportion.
Gravity and time's distortion will make them atone.

Mary has a severe home-brew habit, so is known as 'The Mother of Grog'. I chart a wide berth down the tiled aisle; she gives me her tired, wonky, sad smile. I grin politely for a while, and throw a sort of flirty wave to the well-plied, preening, graceless trio as I cruise past, starboard side. Keeping options open for a different leaning, spring tide, or raging storm when any port is required.

'Steady as she blows!'...

Lawrence Reed.

Excerpt 2 from the epic poem The Barricade.

Joining the gamblers... I get in pint **six** ('half a dozen!') of The Best in on my jackeroo, squiffy, pondering what the sodding hell to do, before plodding stiffly over to a fanatical gambling group of iffy bent brothers I often ally. Set on the whiffy, spiralling, sticky carpet in the Saloon's salubrious quarter: the old 'card room'. The intertwining tendrils of blue-grey fag smoke rising up through the chandelier lighting could be almost beautiful if they were something else:

>votive incense or sacrificial smoke.

A lone, etiolated palm suffers softly in an alcove. Palm leaves: the ancient symbol of victory with integrity.

They could not be more out of place.

Cards slip and whisper on the emerald baize, displaying the periodic shifts of power. I observing the human hands holding the card hands and wonder which have more life. The gambler's hands have their own revealing details; like a facial physiognomy they can be read. While the playing card's vibrant patterns are always different; living each night in infinite unreadable combinations.

Tonight, I just monitor maliciously, praising their haphazard logic. Their regular circular table has a lower platform to put booze and blazing fags; so the surface is unsullied. Not the usual ring-stains rippling from different sized glasses like a small pool in a faint rain shower. Around it sit the irregular pentad of Punters: Amazing Andrew of the anchovy-aura ('half-seas-over', wrecked), crouching with pessimistic Philip, lazy Bartholomew, ex-tearaway Thomas and crazy Thaddeus.

All nicely pissed.

>Set in a chain-smoking icy mist.

They all indulge in some clandestine form of the blustering Brag. Descendent of vile Primero. I know it well, it's addictive and pernicious. I initiate: "Hi, here's mud in yer eye!" Gamblers reply: "Hi mate, fancy a try at the Melvyn?"

I sigh, wondering under my breath... "Why?"

'Almighty Andy' has a randy braggart's bearing made for the game. Twin talents: bullshitter and card-counter. X-certificate warning on his wrist. Andy has the long, elegant fingers of a virtuoso which he meticulously cricks after quickly picking out ill begotten spoils. Typical anxious ectomorph's trick, divulging his wicked streak. Each finger, except the foreshortened pinkie, boasts a fine gem-stone ring. He claims he hears each cut crystal singing with its own special vibrations.

Phil's solid. Big raw heart. Pessimistic player so plots an even keel. Adores the odds like me, keeps it real; smart strategy. He caresses his cards with the soft, supple-skin hands of an office worker which belie a soft strength. Well-proportioned digits but, for early winter, unnaturally over-suntanned. The tell-tale white band on the ring finger. Gold annulus secreted in waistcoat pocket, temporarily obsolete. A craftily planned double bluff, like his best card playing.

Deceit upon vulpine deceit.

Signs for all to understand. In short,

the hands of a grand, loveable, shameless

cheat.

Phil doesn't know who his father was but a big family man himself (when he's not apart, pubbing) with two lovely girls. The fucker struck lucky in so many ways. I'm not saying my life sucks, but I wonder dreamily... could I seriously aspire to that one day? No way.

Not 'stuck in this rut' anyway.

Maybe I should pray?

Phil's new mate Bartholomew beams radioactively; bang out of his ebrious skin. He has no hint of guile in him: saintly, too innocent to win, doomed to be flayed alive. He grins when he has a good hand so, of *course, everyone folds. Hands with the shrivelled lizard-like skin of a light-dodging troglodyte. Pasty white. Aged in a different timeframe to his face, despite incongruously manicured nails. The thumbs look barely opposable, slightly vestigial. There's a faint scar between the index finger and the extraordinarily elongated middle finger of both hands, betraying the blight of a primeval, webbed, piscine heritage. Frightfully fishy, right?*

He's what we call a 'pot monkey' and usually departs the Brag soon after Tom. Bar means 'son of' and he truly strives to be 'a son of the Bar'. Stares and stares unblinkingly as if looking at some invisible work of abstract art, or out-of-focus eye chart. I never could say what that stare meant; it make me uneasy. Consummate big-hearted arsehole. Known to us by far more nicknames than our genital parts. 'Two-hat Nat', 'Spare Part Bart', 'Bar-Bar, and 'Bart the Farter', that's just for starters...
and, as if on cue, he lets rip. Wey-hay!

Inexplicably loyal Tom is a short ex-tearaway, round and ever so unsound. On the boil. Well clear of the mark. Emotionally on the rebound, which he underplays. Sparky. Small, red splodge on his forehead; a cursed birthmark. Broad-flanged nose with the texture of an over-ripened plum. Closet Hemingway fan. But living one of his hero's dark, boozy holidays instead of a great-white shark hunt. Prone to 'throw a wobbler'. Emits a coiled restless energy all around, like a hunting hound before the chase gets underway; eased by nervy origami. Uses his mound of found materials: beer mats, crisp packets and painstakingly unwound bottle-foil;
then folds them into mutant animal forms for some diabolical ark
    or freakish theme park.

    As Tom clutches his pint glass he proudly displays the bruised and calloused hands of a manual labourer; rough to the touch with thick blue bulging veins, rising from the anaemic skin, that visibly pulse. Fingers hooked into a stiff claw from too much abuse, as if premature rigor mortis has set in. An old accident has made the index and middle fingers of his righthand look cartoonishly crooked. A recent wound is oozing. Bandages of any sort proffered by Ve, are naturally refused.

Waxen-faced chain-smoker with a piled ashtray. Passing the time of day. Smells of stale Indian take-away. Left leg pounds up and down making an utterly annoying racket, betraying the stuttering, asymmetric rhythms of his anxious card-play (an infectious twitch which I pick up). This son of a bitch is extremely skittish today.
I'm in no doubt his bluffs will be laid bare
       as the London clay at the bottom of an empty grave.

Tom often asks me: "Where are we bound this night?" (Quite a sound-bite.) I always politely answer: "On the way to the truth and light." He doubts my wisdom but it's only a sick joke, right?
    Struth.

    Thaddeus, known by the misnomer of 'Sane Jude' is another Billingsgate boy; crude, sullen and rude. Shuffling the pack with his short stubby fingers: retarded evolutionary throwbacks that look like they only have two phalanges. Symbols of his hard endomorphic physiology. Shouting the right message in the brutal Brag but becoming clumsy in games involving holding more cards. Hands that convey a guarded truth: bulbous and scarred boxer's knuckles, which he used profusely in his youth. A gold-plated, ruthless cunt.

Short and stout like the toby jugs. Napoleon complex. Poker-faced fascist. Dangerously devout. Gives me the evil eye and shrugs. Flouts any manners. His lower lip pouts like a trout and glistens with brownish saliva. A shady sad-clown variant. Joints riddled with his latest bout of gout but sit's bolt upright with oddly immaculate posture. Spouts dry flannel through the lefthand corner of his mouth. Hates Europe and the 'Brussel sprouts' (bad shout). Touts Thatcher. Borderline pseudo N.F. lout but can't stand the Krauts. Vents lies upon bent lies without showing a shadow of a doubt. By-

the-by he plays the Brag pretty well, unlike his darts, where rebounding flying arrows have nearly taken his 'mince pies' out.

Tonight the boys are high in febrile spirits. Opaque smiles, opaquer fates, slyly scratching balding blistered crowns. Heads stay looking down, loosely hinged leaden weights. Waiting, bowed in prayer. All-knowing nods with concentrated deep-ploughed frowns. Quivers and trembles abound; clear signs around to those allowed to decipher. 'Thou shalt not cheat': a commandment they deviously disavow.
Rugged brows wait for a sacrificial cow...
    How now?

I sit on a random stool guileful-glancing at trying Tom's crap pair of fives trying not to 'let the cat out the bag'. He's bluffing and going to 'get taken for a good ol' ride'. He picks his nose then furtively slides his hand to scratch chronic stigmata on his prickly, itchy side; telling tics he pitifully hides. 'Thick as a nine-inch brick'; he doesn't grasp the rules, probabilities or wider tactics. Can't kick his horizonless losing streak. This prick cannot 'Adam and Eve' the others' skill (or luck), convinced they're cheating sods up to crafty tricks; or the cards are not fickle but fixed. A doubting dick checking for firm attestation: from insisting on breaking the seal on a virgin pack, to surveying the deck at the end... classic. 'Gets on everyone's wick' but adds to the pot then gets out quick. Shies his rounds; always brassic.

Cleaned out by Andy's hot three sixes, Tom's ill-fated chair is vacated. He totters off to rot, speared and instantly forgot. The Brag-gang desires another clot. I seriously consider, then spurn the offer. Not tonight. Far too tight to give a jot. They berate my sad state but it's really not my turn to take. Lost the plot. Matthias, whom I've never met, replaces Tom, unprecedentedly chosen by some kind of covert lot. A new overt sot. Slaps down his stake in the starter pot. Guess what? Goes: "Two quid blind." I was right. He's predictably shite. Dot, dot, dot.

The gambling's usually fairly tame, only spasmodically gets inflamed. Should be banned. What I never, ever, understand is how you often lose the most money with your best hand! There's a damned screwed-up metaphor for life all right!
Mirroring my odyssey, stormy waters,

> *not as simple as planned on first sight*

Rod's husky, anthemic melody propels me onwards alone. We Are Sailing. I raise an imaginary ensign:

> *the fair skull and cross bones of the corsairs...*

Lawrence Reed.

A Slug in the Milk.

It was a cold wet kiss,
Unwelcome, invasive,
So unexpected,
Probing and tapping,
At my lips.

When you take a sneaky slug,
From the milk bottle,
Instead of glass, cup or mug,
Don't complain or be surprised,
When a sluggish kiss awaits inside!

Alexander Joe Walsh.
(August 2021)

Despicable Beings.

They are despicable beings,
But don't call them that!
It might hurt their feelings,
To expose their leanings.

They are despicable beings,
Who eat their own parents,
And cannibalise meanings,
Then spew incestuous doctrines.

Opposites attract against the odds,
One bad turn deserves a pat on the back!
Money banks for the fat-cats,
Food banks for the middle-class.
Heat banks, WTF, who saw that side ball?
Who saw that coming – own up!

Smirking imbeciles run the asylum,
Yes, they really did take over.
Borrowing is good,
Except it's not when you're poor.

But all people were born equal?
I don't think so!
All people become equal though!
Do you think so?
But some people become even more equal,
Than others, as we know!

Alexander Joe Walsh.
(October 2022)

Vampires.

There are vampires here,
And they feel no fear,
Of the daylight anymore.

They live above us,
And all around us,
And they move amongst us.

They glide like white sharks,
Searching in curves and arcs,
Through empty eyes.

They are sly creatures!
They don't seem like leeches,
But they really are.

They are shape shifters,
And faithless drifters,
In cocktail dress and business suit.

And they will suck you,
And they will drain you,
And they will bleed you,
Dry.

Alexander Joe Walsh.
(October 2022)

The Big Thing Thit's Iverywhere.

She said, "Ye ken, its yon big thing. The big thing thit's iverywhere! Ye cannie see it close up. Ye wid ken it. I jist cannie mind what it's cawed!" She sat for a moment thinking, trying tae recall what the big thing thit wis iverywhere wis cawed. I sat thinking while she tried tae regain her train o' thought. I couldnae fathom what she could be meaning, or what she wis trying tae remember. What was big and iverywhere?

We were in oor other sister's flat in Dumbryden, on the Murrayburn Road edge o Westerhailes in Edinburgh. I was visiting fae where I live in Aberdeenshire. As soon as the covid restrictions relaxed enough for me tae visit, I packed a bag and took off south in my van wi my wee dug. As I drove across the new 'Brig O Harps', and ower the slate grey Firth O' Forth wi Edinburgh in the distance, I gloried in my new freedom. Arthur's Seat crouched in the distance, beholding the ancient place o my birth. My hert fluttered and my stomach did a somersault, even at my age.

I looked oot the kitchen windae, through the trees opposite the tenement, and ower the red tiled roofs o' the hooses across the busy road. It was sae fine tae be there, within shouting distance o where ten o' us were brought up in oor three bedroom cooncil hoose.

"Sometimes it isnae awfy nice, in fact it can be horrible. Other times it's lovely," she explained, shaking her heid. She battled wi' the Alzheimer's and her face went red, she wis embarrassed at being unable tae say what it wis. I thought for a second that she was gaun tae greet. But she didnae. She composed herself, held on tae her dignity. She dis everything wi' dignity though, she ay his, aw the hard stuff. She wis annoyed wi herself. Annoyed wi herself for not being able tae remember this thing that she wanted tae tell me aboot. The big thing thit's iverywhere. We were sitting at oor sister's kitchen table, drinking coffee and jist enjoying being able tae see each other, and speak tae each other again efter sich a long time. Except it wis hard for her tae jist speak when she forgot what words she wanted tae use. Hard tae jist talk casually and say what she wanted tae say. Tae talk aboot not very much. Nothing important. Just tae talk wi her brother, and chew the fat while their sister cooked fish and tatties for the tea. She looked oot the windae wi hard fought concentration on her face. "Sometimes it's grey like the day. Look!" she exclaimed, and nodded towards the windae in triumph. I followed her nod and gazed through the big pane o' glass at the grey sky, and there it was, the big thing thit's iverywhere.

Alexander Joe Walsh.
(March 2022)

Frida Kahlo.
Frida Kahlo kissed me
Under the mistletoe
She delicately whispered in my ear
Then said she had to go
I felt her fingers slip from mine
I fell backwards, back in time
Frida Kahlo kissed me
Adios she said I have to fly

Frida Kahlo's fragile smile
Almost missing, almost mist
She blew her kiss to land upon my lips
Then discretely turned to take her leave
I felt the wind caress my face
I sensed the magic that she traced
Frida Kahlo's fragile smile
Almost missing as she turned to mist

Frida Kahlo's immortal look
Caught in colours neath moonlights glow
Her fingers craft her spiritual art
With heavenly grace she ascends and flows
The wind blew her pure kiss to my cheek
Which burned my skin with sensual pain
Frida Kahlo's immortal look
Adios she said as she rose to leave

Frida Kahlo kissed me
Frida Kahlo kissed me
Frida Kahlo kissed me under the mistletoe!

Seamus McLeod.
(October 2022)

The Place Of Correction.
Try to forget all that you've learned from your introduction to time
All that's before you will mould you and manipulate your mind
Oh yes, there may be singing and dancing and merriment
Just don't you dance to a different tune
Oh, and by the way, you can forget all that sentiment
You won't be rising to any old fool's moon

This is a place of correction for people like you
By the time that we leave you'll be people like us
Unless of course you don't adhere to the system
And you have dreams that your life is some kind of mission
No, you don't have the capacity for original thought
And we might just arrange for you to be untaught

Oh, they tell us that your father has his head up his arse
He's been listening to Lenin, Mao and Marx
Well, we have other ideals that we feed to fools like you
And our mantra is obedience to the royal family of rules
So, we will ready you for a life of "Do as you're told"
Whilst we shape you and shorn you as sheep for the fold

This is a place of correction for people like you
When the time comes to leave, you'll be people like us
So, don't listen to hot air that blows like a horn in the fog
Whilst we fine tune your actions to that of a well-trained dog
Don't go thinking your life is something, it's not worth a jot
And we have procedures for editing out what you've caught

So, we're tracking your progress, we're writing it down
We won't let errors of judgement loosen our grip on the crown
Our agents will collect you from the lost and found
We don't want unwelcome influence finding fertile ground
And so, if we must we will break your mostrenco streak

And remind you of whose words to say when you speak
This is a place of correction for people like you
And when the time comes to leave, you'll be people like us
Oh, but you're not responding, your seeds from stubborn stock
While time is running down on your astronomical clock
Just one more step as you edge towards the brink
And we have arrangements to unfasten the link

You're pulling away in a divergence of rays
While the curtain comes down on what remains of your days
You may cling to the ring of the promise of youth
But by your two left feet we have uncovered the truth
Now may be the time to throw you to the dogs
And lay you to rest neath the age-old peat bogs

This is a place of correction for people like you
And by the time that you leave you should be people like us
But if there's no way we can train your brain to our thoughts
Then we'll pull all the strings to have you tied up in knots
You're just a radical particle on a collision course with time
We're now taking action to leave you behind

Now I look back on the days that came before the nights
And I struggle with concepts beneath this great arc of lights
I may be a pioneer travelling from the source of my pain
But its powerful presence will forever remain
They tempt me to return to the "Power and the Glory"
But each turn of the page repeats the same old story

There stands the place of correction for people like me
And at the time of my leaving, I'm not sure that I am free
I visit the temples and I drink with the saints
Who are safely concealed beneath ten coats of paint
I stand in the sunshine and I hold out my hands

But in the back of my mind a dark shadow hangs
There stands the place of correction for people like me
And the closer I look the less that I see.

Seamus McLeod.
(October 2022)

What I Notice Most!
I've been down to the end of a one-way street
With a noose around my neck
I don't want to talk about it all that much
It's an act I'd best forget
I see the mark left by the rope
I brush it off with laughter
Then scale the walls to find new hope
And cover up the mark that's left there

I'm seeking God in a dark blue sky
Orion's right there on my shoulder
I feel the force behind my eyes
I've never been down this road quite so far
But where is this voice coming from
There's no one standing here!
Should I venture back into the room
Where the darkness hides my tears?

The crisp cold touch of winters light
Attacks my shrinking body
I could easily disappear from sight
Tonight, and then tomorrow
If no one comes to look for me
Then will I still be missing?
There's more to ponder than to see
I'm leaking hear me hissing!

What I notice most is silence
As life goes on and on and on
In black and white ambivalence
The cracks are there for all to see
They're just too blind to notice
I'm slowly turning into stone

It may take some time
But eventually I'll get there!

Seamus McLeod.
(October 2022)

Slava Ukraini!
there is only us and them
beneath the shells
and bloodied skies
where no birds fly
and the air is heavy
with the smells
of death
there is only us and them
a sundered brotherhood
and treaties denied
cleft by empirical levy
behest by despots
breath
there is only us and them
the sunflower
and the bear
we have the strength
of righteous power
they are the invader
we shall devour
there is only us and them
until
there is only
us.

Andy Greenhouse.

Who Am I Deluding?

Been to the gym
For a swim
To keep my body working
Keeping trim.

On the yoga mat
With my Jazzy Cat
Doing some Pilates
To keep my tummy flat.

Walking and a-hiking
Cycling and a-rowing
To keep the O2 flowing
And my muscles showing.

But my mirror keeps belying
"Girl you are a -lying!
Why, you're not even trying!
Why are you denying?"

Who am I deluding?

Janette Fenton.

When Autumn Leaves Fall.

Autumn dew drops
On Passion Fruit leaves
Serve as water stations
For thirsty birds and bees
And crawlies
That visit for a sip
As autumn leaves slip
Down from bush and tree
To fresh cut lawns
And still warm streets
That prepare to meet
Autumn's chill.

In autumn's breeze
They float and fall
And enthral
Free-falling parachutes
Sway this way and that
They meet and mingle
Rustle and chat
Couple and uncouple
And sprinkle a riot of yellow and red
Onto grey pavements.

When autumn leaves fall
Nature showers the land with colour
And hearts with awe.

Janette Fenton.

I Missed The Sun Today.

I missed the sun today
Because I got carried away
While writing a poem about a spider.
I told myself to abandon the laptop
Get pad and pen
Sit in the garden
Instead, the words kept flowing
Spinning a word thread-
A spider diagram
In my head
Mind- mapping my poem.
So industrious was my flow
How could I interrupt it so
Just leave and go?
No!
Not even for the sunniest glow
On this illuminated day
I decided to stay
Until I finished my poem
Then catch some rays
But that didn't happen today
As words kept flooding onto my Word page.

Janette Fenton.

Spider On The Wire.

The tightrope crawler

Crafts a magnificent wire of silk

Super strong, sticky silk.

She releases it from the Eucalyptus tree twig to my washing line

In a diagonally, perfected incline

Of skyscraper proportion

Paced and measured in spider counts

Strung high.

She mounts.

Her creation floats on a slither of air

And deftly, with the skill of a tightrope walker

She fearlessly ferries underside across her creation

No balancing pole in sight

For the upside-down stalker

Back and forth

Effortlessly

Industriously

Spinning

Until she completes her task.

In the autumn sunlight

Her wire glints like a blade

Her silk thread gleams and shimmers

Silver and orange through my windowpane
A meteor rain tube in the sun
While she hides in the shade-
She waits.

Soon there will be blood on this wire
The arachnid is ready.

Janette Fenton.

Should We Let The Treasures Sleep?

Should we resurrect the treasures
That lie like shipwrecks
At the bottom of the sea?
Clean them up and restore them
Put on show for all to see
Or should we leave them be?
For centuries
For fear that time will alter
And erode their significance
Become irrelevant
In a modern world.

Should we let the treasures sleep?
In the dark and hidden deep
When the past has said goodbye
Is it time to let them die?

Janette Fenton.

From The Pulpit.

The Sunday ritual never changed
The preacher of the Free Church of Scotland would raise his voice
Tones of condemnation and wrath would vibrate throughout the sculpted pulpit,
The pulpit that condemned sin.

From the pulpit, the preacher strived in vain
In God's name
To herd his wayward flock from plunging
Into the pit of hell
To prevent them from fleeing like lemmings
Blindly taking a headlong leap of no faith
Into Satan's eternal realm of evil and suffering-
The mouth of hell awaited them.
But, from the pulpit, the shepherd could be their saviour
If only they could hear.

He'd bang his fist on the bible
The bible basher.
"Repent!"
Repeating words from Genesis
That told tales of man's corruption
God's disappointment in his creation

Paths of salvation

For the faithless and lost souls to tread.

The startled congregation

Would flinch

And winch

As he drummed home his message to the sinners

"Repent!

Or damnation awaits you."

They'd lower their heads in guilt

Guilt that multiplied

And amplified from the pulpit.

They clutched repent

And wore it

Like fire-blankets

To prevent

The flames and brimstone

From singeing

Their layers of transgression

For fear of retribution

In the pit of hell.

Janette Fenton.

Big Fish/Little Fish.

Plenty of moving objects in the sky, eclipsing lights
And stars and junk
Here on earth if that's where we are, primates changing
Odourless toxic gas, brain and other vital
Organs deprived of oxygen
Without vision we'd lose consciousness, spied on from
High above indiscernible heights
To capture big fish little satellites are born, feeding off little
Fish, small fry from unexplored oceans
Seldom gazed at celestial movement, an early oeuvre of Explosive
psychic overtures
Music for the planets to evade Elon Musk, parasitic
Entrepreneurs and their ilk
Genres worse than show business defiling Marilyn Monroe, net
Worth an attic filled with iconic sluttery, our leader's
Adultery well documented, attributed to different days
Pawns escaping capture as Europe's war stretches beyond the Pale,
televised live hourly
Makes our lives seem inconsequential
Loop-the-loop, Crazy Horse back on the grind, one fell swoop
Giving it Lulu, catalysts born with Aspergers, autism competes
With the signs to look for
And all of these foibles, an astronaut punching a conspiracist's
Facial theory
Molten rock set against paper trees and sonic steel, it gets worse
Nostalgia buckles to drunken binges, synthesised images
And an eclipsed nuclear oasis
The blinding deafness turns back time for an hour, nostalgia's Way
of harming conscious trees, there's something about
Each life sentence that doesn't sit right
Upon vacant thrones, imbalance of power
All the world's illnesses rolled into one virus, the entire world's
violence riddled through a continuum.

Cue the vaccinated scaremongers, their task to dupe
The masses
Unable and not allowed to travel, these simple minds
Usurp great thinkers; rob organic soil for killer cures
All we revellers want is to dance, to forget our surrogate dues
More billionaires now than at any other time, cashing in on
Crashing markets, failing economies
And feigned interest in fossil fuel
No margin for error, no error for profit
Lies harmful when breathed, when believed
Suffocated at birth, bred for wealth, minds poisoned
Limbs disabled, artificial intelligence at minimal cost
Let all these young teams be heard, printed
Hinting at an answers, positive solutions, your Greta Thunbergs
And your Young Activists UK (British Visitors need not apply)
Vote for *Effie*
Vote for *Common Sense*
Vote for *Socialism*
Vote for *Investment*
Disguise our discuss at obscene dividends paid to shareholders,
These self-proclaimed owners of this raped orb, shatter
The myths, these despicable borders
This land is free, rid of us
This land is evolving, we must leave it as we found it
Let Ulysses return home, and catch sight of this historical
Homecoming.

Meek.

She Looks Up.

She looks up
the carvings on the temple ceiling
seem to breathe
she stares hard to fix them with her eyes

as she tips back her head
something falls from her
and wonder floods through her
suddenly she is a girl again
dizzy with rapture
walking on a river that at any moment
might drown her in delight

from time to time
in your life
you will have cause to look up
and the river will appear before you.

Jon Bickley.

That Smile.

We sat on a balcony in Florence

a city so beautiful that even the dust in the street

causes you to catch your breath

coming as it does from Michelangelo's studio.

The sunlight bounced off the walls

danced on the river and sang in the street.

We drank coffee and then you smiled

and I never saw Florence again.

Jon Bickley.

Age.

In a quiet street the shadows touch and
darkness flows around you, dragging you down.
Age rests its hand on your shoulder and you
stumble, not knowing what is happening.
Age does not come quietly in ones and twos
but in press gangs to haul you off to sea
never to feel the certainty of dry
land again. Never to trust your own feet.
It beats you and steals from you everything
you never thought about before. Walking,
seeing, hearing, dancing, wooing and loving.
A changeling switched in the darkness where your
memory used to be. A pig in a coat
good for nothing but dreams and poetry.

Jon Bickley.

The First Time.

The first time that I saw you
my eyes were fixed
I couldn't look away
a black sun brooding, intense, wonderful,
books spilling from the crook of your arm
your jersey stretched across your breasts
an eruption of hair

The first time I heard you
words tumbled out all at once
volcanic
not completely trusting what was happening
ideas chasing each other
to the top of the glass and bursting out
How dare Hardy objectify Tess like that?

The first time I touched you
we sat together on a couch
and we leaned towards each other
an electrical circuit was completed
and warmth hummed into being
something happened that happened
only occasionally later.
Later, when we lay naked and panting
it was not the same.

The first time was a voice calling
Come Home

The first time I smelled you
was in Norfolk I think
smell is mysterious, elusive
hard to detect and harder to remember
I remember sea air, wood smoke
lavender but there was something else
you thought we could be just friends
that smell laid another trail.

The first time I tasted you
The first time?
How am I meant to remember the first time?
Probably Florence, I don't know.
The bubbles rush to the top of the champagne flute
and burst in my face
the taste of the world
the deep, dark, volcanic earth
my tongue lifting the hood
touching the bud
juices swallowed
flooding all over my face
dripping from my chin
Rain forests, rivers, tall trees

parrots, unnameable creatures
in the undergrowth
unseeable mysteries
swimming against the tide
pushing on until I heard
the same rush and bubble
of sensations I had once heard
everything happening at once
a volcanic rush
of joyous noise
as below and so above.

Jon Bickley.

Marie Musters Me Her Fragile Delicate Dress.

Marie musters me her fragile

delicate dress.

She tells me

I am a person of coincidence.

Legs wild,

eyes distilled by darkness

she puts her head between the wheels.

Taking notes from old diaries,

darkness frames this cool conception.

While counting the minutes

on the clock.

Groundless,

Mindless,

I turn to secure the door.

I make sure.

Then I go back to the stencil,

heat becomes the sinner

and my body cowers

to a more accepted form of sleep.

Giancarlo Moruzzi.

Profile.

The changeling walks

the wall of death.

Dangerous,

forbidden,

fingers grow talons

in the wired night.

Wingless angels mutate

while poet's cry.

Barefoot spies

tattooed,

sinful,

hide in jewelled prisons.

Rooftop icon

Howling at midnight,

delicate tears

disappear in the mist.

The actors have all gone

you are alone,

you thought you had it made

but that's not why you are here,

that's not why you joined

this mad parade.

Giancarlo Moruzzi.

Forest.

The mist has taken

the trees hostage,

while animals do

their dance of death,

in wild desperate forests.

We are just helpless observers

to the changes

that are coming.

The winds' skeletal fingers

wrapped around

the throat of earths' tranquillity.

It never rains in this darkness

only fire prevails,

ships struggling in the oceans

along with their burning sails.

Giancarlo Moruzzi.

Anticipation.

The soldiers of dawn

Stand ready to bury

The past remnants of night,

dressed

in pale tired armour,

whispering secret passwords

that can never be repeated.

Tired sisters wait

at some random quay side,

ashtrays full of memories

ready to accept

the inevitable.

Starlings fly in an

ominous sky

their tears

wash through the clouds,

that break the dawn.

Giancarlo Moruzzi.

Night.

Night,

the fat parasite,

the blind man's symphony

that seems so right.

Giancarlo Moruzzi.

New Direction.

Tonight

we look at the ocean,

from frozen hill tops,

ruined pyramids steeped

in soured dreams.

Wounded and miserable

legs bound,

lost hitchhikers

speaking in new languages,

waiting for desolate cars

to take them away

to start again

under a new direction.

Giancarlo Moruzzi.

Ghosts.

Ghosts

sit like water

on the hunched shoulders

of burnt-out heroes.

The tired night

whispers

to the TV bed.

Sun bleached madness

allows you to travel

through your imagination.

Stay awake

and close your eyes.

Wait in vain

for the ultimate surprise.

Giancarlo Moruzzi.

Needs And Wants.

Always at odds
Leave it in the hands of the gods.
Mind blank, now it's racing
Like a caged animal
Always pacing

Night, day
Tidy, disarray
Constant chatter,
Nothing to say

Way in front,
Falling behind,
Welcome to my crazy mind.

Susan Broadfoot.

Fortune And Fame.

May be to blame

But You've changed .....

Things will

Never be the same

'Cos You've changed ......

Where did you go

Or are you just hiding

into another world you are sliding

Is there any point in looking for you

Are you happy with the things that you do?

Give me your trust

talk to me

I'm still here ....

Tell me your secrets

Cry if you must

I'm still here .....

It's plain to see your life is tough

But where is that person I knew?

You have to say when you've had enough

And just be you

You've changed

You've changed
You've changed.

Susan Broadfoot.

Look At Me.

Look at me
I am free
My own being
Comfortable in my own skin
Where I should always have been
A new way of seeing

Unlike any other
Ok a bit like my mother
But what does that make me
Different, unique?
Do I need a label?
A monster or a freak?

No, no, no
Because we are individually made
So, so, so
Don't be scared to stand against the grade
you see
You just need to be, be, be
Just be.

Susan Broadfoot.

Shitsville UK.

Things are getting drastic

We're awash in sewage and plastic

Our lovely coastal towns

With beaches golden brown

Are now a sad reflection

Of mass produced infection

Relax back on you lilo

And drift right out to sea

On waves of dirty nappies

Full of shit and pee

Sitting on your deck chair

Relaxing in the heat

As Neptune washes up

Used tampons round your feet

The seagulls have gastritis

The rats have all left town

It's enough to make a copraphiliac

Frown

A tidal wave of coke tins

Clatter round your ears

A diarrhoea flavoured slush puppy
Confirms your worst fears

You've saved your pennies all year round
To have a cosy break
But one hour in Shitsville-on-Sea
And you know it's a mistake.

Mark Ingram.
(04.11.2022)

November.

November, November, remember remember,
Remember, remember in November.
The sadness, the pain, the loss, all remain
Lingering around the restless brain.
But as each night has its day
And each Fall has its Spring.
So, this November will have its May!

November.
What do you grieve, my friend?
What hurt and loss burdens your soul?
Me? I, myself grieve, I mourn - the deaths of five,
Of Family friends and acquaintances.
The unjustness of politics, the desertions of a child,
The premature halt to an artistic venture...
I grieve... I find my way to deal and hide and cope...
Health and mind battle against all these odds
With poison and sleep and walks and ...
Hope - there will be may be May, I hope.

May.
My pal Martin, the Warrior, sadly one of the losses
Positive ever and defied poor health
With gratitude for all the goodness
To be found in everydayness.

May. May I too, be grateful for such blessing.
To live and have shelter and creature comforts.
I may not have all that I desire,
But I have and I am - and may
I be ever so.
So, may this be a tribute to him.
May, May be on our horizons
This dark, cold November,
That pain will have joy and cold the heat
With loss a gain, elixir for the pain.

Now.
May you no not remember
That which makes you strong.
Dig deep and see your soul
And welcome the Ying to your Yang
Your joy to your pang.
This to all and all gratitude.

Niamh Mahon.

The Fire Of Oblivion.

What burns first in the fire of Oblivion?

We were children and we were crossing three mountains on the only path, there was a sleeping snake

We were scared but we had no choice, we jumped over it in terror when we turned around to see it it got up and jumped up

up into the tree

What burns first in the fire of oblivion? The imaginary life?

The snake was waiting for us, all is one language

that cannot be communicated

Why does it burn imaginary life first? Because this is real life

The fire of Oblivion burns what cannot be burned Conscious life is a shape

like the shadows of the trees at night. It is a reflection arbitrary

It is a parchment that is written

of animal traces that run in the night. Maybe we should hide in it

The imaginary life returns?

Constantly in myriad forms of the subconscious anxious for the new form it will take

Why does it burn the imaginary life? Because human memory is a tiny microcosm the excrement of an exiled herd

Because imaginary life has no memory what it is, it is always shared the snake was waiting for us

jumped ten feet high to the top of the tree In imaginary life, lightning burned the tree, we slept at its root

where the snake seemed to sleep

instead of us

It was the one time

that the imaginary life was not burned

That's why I can talk to you now.

George Bakolas.

PANK's Not Dead.

Yes, I know, my dear once a Punk

said to a lady with blue pearls

on her beautiful cavernous breasts I'll spit in your graves

No, he didn't mean it. What he meant to say

It was about the scar . . . The deep scar on the face of decency

Don't take it personally But, you know, decency is a very bad thing

Don't put on any more makeup Civilization is a bridge

that you have to allow everyone to cross If there are crocodiles in the river

have human limbs for lunch

Sorry, sir . . . I don't want to know you Punk wasn't a collection culture

It was never a rating fund

Punk was the withering away of the human earth just before it finally died

before he could see a red flower with yellow boots dancing

like a crazy wild goat on the edge of a cliff the Punk went across

He made the incredible leap into eternity. Not of music

Not of protest. Not of revolution

but the recording of a hopeless event of adolescence as the only testimony

of the unique contemplation without words for what he cried out, the words

do not hear it

the arts do not pack it in boxes. He screamed of destruction

Of the most basic thing

The only oxygen

on the martyred bottom of the dark riddle of life youth

Youth like a warm snowstorm that freezes time

and dances furiously on the lava

Of all the volcanoes that haunt existence just before the ice melts

and the lost Atlantis appears of the civilization of fears enclosed within the squares

of the homes of the workplaces

leave the Punk on the naked highway confounding the human lizards

and laughs spontaneously At sunset

That will be a little while longer

For his sake.

George Bakolas.

Turkey.

There is a sadness in people when they see the cursed ones

When you're wearing a red dress

When the polished shoe

Fall in love with a white dust

When the teenager works

When the beloved becomes a firework

When the faucet stops dripping drops

When birds stand still above the crowd

When the streets distract the future from the past

When everything happens because loneliness cannot wait

No carriage no train

And just climbs the ladder

There's a joy in people

When they lick the ice cream with hot fudge

When they open the umbrella

When they dance without any music when they say their name

And bow to their wrist

When they make love

straight without seeing anyone's body

When they dream of spring

In poor streets

when they love what is given to them when they die while smiling

when they live with the hidden meaning

No matter if they know it

When they grow up like children when they swim forgetting their breath

When they believe that the gift

Will be sent forever

especially when they are crushed with joy

And mistake it for this pride of the turkey

that thrills as it exists

there on the edge of the all-white morning of memory

Of glory that never grows old of the mirror

that, broken, sticks again when all is in tatters.

George Bakolas.

Jack Kerouac.

It's hard to say something about grief without fearing that it might

of hurting a running horse on the distant steppe

Yes, I'm saddened by "THE ROAD"

It's running me over with its wheels

And brakes on the cliff

Is that true

But the teenager is fascinated by heights

The intricate web of escape

From a prison without a name with no identity and no end

The girls sit on the hood of the Mustang the desert laughs with its yellow teeth the fox dances with the cobra

Let's go, Jack says to the girls

But he's alone

How the horizon has grown, he says

Yesterday it was closer

The further you go, the more you learn

Not to count

The man escaped from the war

The war hid in his pocket

The workers have no country.

While they're young, they don't die.

Dreams die before they do.

America is a difficult birth

The children will go to school

They will love and be loved America is a difficult birth

Don't wish it on anyone

♪ Grow up fast ♪

So fast that their horizon crosses the earth

before they themselves can to feel its soil

Jack saw a lot of lightning that day and said let's go see the fires.

if the gasoline doesn't get there we'll spread our wings.

George Bakolas.

Anna Karenina.

Anna Karenina did not live in this life but in the one Tolstoy chose for her.

There, amidst a network of intricate transmissions of life, she fought honestly to become part of her. But she was not real, that is, human,

she was unreal, that is, capable of all these things. that the author proposed and she did.

Of course, it's not about romance. It's never about romance.

For Anna Karenina it was about possibility.

of expectation, the garment of the carefree soul.

the transcendence as a means to all that she envisioned.

But the content, this material that overwhelms the soul like the morning fragrance of blossoming gardens

in this paradise that shocks the revelation of more than the impossibility of its realization Anna Karenina fought in the Roman arena of human futility, naked and alone.

none of the people around her understood anything.

From the bottom that shook the surface of her life.

She was a prey for the many. a vision for the few.

She believed in the idea of absolute existence. in that she had no experience.

No true man,

that's why she didn't live among us. Like a doll in a window of sighs.

of our mediocre and futile sorrow when she left behind her a speck of a transparent, soft as breath, look... sometimes you find it in some people. Especially those who, on the occasion of love.

They transform for a moment.
into the hero of this book he's writing. only once in a while.
Anna Karenina
who became an author
and then mentions your name
and you become part of the tragedy too.

George Bakolas.

"KLEOS"

The crew of the boat was not afraid
a sailor had taken the little girl in his arms pushing with his feet a broken oar
to throw it overboard
Somewhere once we saw two more boats;
An old woman I'd never seen before on the island
She was betting on who would sink first.

There were thirteen of us all together
The most of us knew each other. The old woman we didn't know two merchants as yellow as the chests they carried
A priest, a cranky priest with a devilish look in his eyes a newly married couple who kept her pregnancy a secret though they all knew it. I who intended to leave forever the sailor with the crying little girl, and his parents who seemed to be coming in for the first time in a boat as they vomited out of it for almost the whole trip.
And a young man who didn't even seem to know the language as he spoke to no one and clutched an empty cage.

The truth is that there were three others but I'm not talking about them.
When the sky turned even darker and from the side of the moon
it was certain that death had begun and was coming I took off my shirt

The old woman laughed sarcastically "You can go for an appetizer," she said, "I wasn't going to fall into the sea."

But then there was a bolt of lightning very close, or so it seemed to me because I was blind
and I knew the light of darkness.
I pulled myself up
all the roar of the abyss
I heard what it said and what it would do I turned
and looked at them.

The sailor was frightened
"Who is it?" he asked as the child clutched his throat
They were all there with the knowledge of the abyss evident "Who do the monsters want?" screamed the old woman
who, strangely enough, had white teeth "Satan is with us," said the priest viciously without fear.
The light had burned the whole of the rear side of my back as I turned towards the sea
I fell in thinking
the tender gaze of a mother
who from the depth of the hidden sun calling my name . . .
KLEOS!

George Bakolas.

Authors -

Lawrence Reed - After studying my masters in music composition I became interested in the rhythms and sounds of words. From there my poetry began. In 2020 a volume of my recent works entitled Earth's Secret Engine was published by Inherit The Earth Publication and is available on Amazon. I live in Bath and draw inspiration from the surrounding nature and the strange thoughts it inspires. I write music and lyrics for the prog-folk band Pagan Harvest and play guitar duets with Fight and Flight.

www.lawrencereed.com

Wendy Webb - Born in the Midlands, home and family life in Norfolk. She edited Star Tips poetry magazine 2001-2021. Published in Indigo Dreams, Quantum Leap, Crystal, Envoi, Seventh Quarry) and online (Littoral Magazine, Autumn Voices, Wildfire Words, Lothlorien, Meek), she was placed First in Writing Magazine's Pantoum poetry competition. She devised new poetry forms (Davidian, Magi, Palindromedary); wrote her father's biography, 'Bevin Boy', and her own autobiography, 'Whose Name Was Wit in Waterr' (title inspired by Keats' grave in Rome). She has attempted many traditional forms and free verse. Favourite poets: Dylan Thomas, Gerard Manley Hopkins, John Burnside, John Betjeman, the Romantic Poets (especially Wordsworth), George Herbert, William Blake, Emily Dickinson, Mary Webb, Norman Bissett, William Shakespeare, the Bible, and the Rubaiyat of Omar Khayyam.

Giancarlo Moruzzi - My name is Giancarlo (known to my friends as John) Moruzzi, I was born in London to Italian immigrant Parents and we worked together in the catering trade. I have always had a passion for music and the blues I play guitar and I collect them. I started writing poetry in my teens and particularly like the classic poets and the beat poets. Some of my favourite poets include William Blake, Charles Baudelaire, Lawrence Ferlinghetti, Arthur Rimbaud and Rupert Brooke and obviously Bob Dylan. I think that passion for either music or art is a companion that remains with you the whole of your life.

Annie Foy - Writes short stories and flash fiction. She enjoys performing her work at spoken word events.

Michelle Carr - I was born and still work and live in Glasgow. When I am not toiling at the office, I paint and write poetry. I love all things creative, from music to art, and I love collaborating with others to bring a creative project to fruition.

Seamus McLeod - Seamus/ James McLeod is taken from his first and middle names. He was born and raised In Edinburgh almost 70 years ago. Most of his working life was spent as an Accountant within a major Housebuilder. Writing songs and poems was an escape from the rigid life spent between ledger lines! This stretched back to his rebellious youth and continues to this day!

David Norris-Kay - David was christened David Austin in 1949, and adopted his writing name with the encouragement of his friend and fellow poet the late Margaret Munro-Gibson (Margaret Hoole) who wrote under her Grandmother's and Mother's maiden names. David now does the same. He started writing poetry in 1967, inspired by Simon and Garfunkel's lyrics. His poetry is lyrical and a lot of it is written in traditional forms, although he also writes in free verse. His free verse poem, 'Butterfly' won first prize in the Salopian Poetry Society's competition in 1981, and his poem 'Autumn's Reflection' won the third prize of £250 in Forward Poetry's competition in 2004. David is divorced and lives happily on his own in Sheffield, Yorkshire, England. He is inspired by his happy 1950s childhood, the natural world, (Especially The Peak District National Park) and his friend's children. He writes mostly poetry, although his 4000 word, supernatural short story 'The Moss Garden' was published twice in 'Monomyth' magazine (Atlantean Publishing) in 1986, and again in 2020. His poetry is widely published in the United Kingdom, Australia, The USA and India. His work has appeared in The National Poetry Anthology and 'Heart Shoots' (IDP) in aid of the Macmillan Cancer Charity. David's 83 page poetry collection 'From Time-Buried Years' (Indigo Dreams Publishing) is available from him for £10 (inc p&p) by emailing davidnorriskay@ymail.com PayPal accepted. He is a member of the ALCS and The Society of Authors.

Niamh Mahon - It's all about the drama. Trained as an actress. Niamh brings a passionate intensity to every role she performs, whether it is Local Councillor, Teacher, Mother or Storyteller. She comes from a large Irish family and maintains her Catholic faith today. She moved to London as an actress appearing on stage and in film. Later she had a very successful career with one of the computer giants of the day. Her switch to teaching was made with the same ambition and achievement when she was head of a junior school. Niamh's analytical thinking and eloquent expression marks her out. Today she lives in Rugeley close to her daughter and grandchildren. She is a town councillor, a teacher and a storyteller. She talks to people and she gets things done.

Stephen Scott – I'm a Glasgow based a self-taught Scottish acrylic artist. I began painting, firstly watercolours and then acrylics, 6 years ago as a hobby. After receiving encouragement from other artists, I began to exhibit my works in several Glasgow venues and Galleries. I've donated artworks to various charities for auction, including Shelter, The British Heart Foundation, and Bread Over Bombs, the Glasgow foodbank charity that I hold close to my heart. My work has been constant to the point that from March 2023 I plan to become a full time artist. As for personal highlights, 4 of my artworks, and 2 written pieces, have been used in the top selling publication 'Ignore Alien Orders', a book about my favourite band The Clash. I've also designed album covers for some bands on the Scottish music scene. I give a nod to artists such as Jack Vettriano,

Banksy, and Ray Lowry as inspirations and drive. I say this honestly that the biggest rewards in my career so far are the amazing artists, art lovers and characters I have met through my art. I quote The Clash's Joe Strummer in saying 'without people you're nothing'. I am about to start a new body of artwork with the intention of taking up offers of exhibiting in England and Ireland later next year. My exhibition 'Against the Grain' is currently on show at Front Room Gallery, Helensburgh, until early November2022.

Alexander Joe Walsh - Is a retired social worker, from Edinburgh, living in Aberdeenshire for the last 25 years. He has finally made time to write from his own unique point of reference.

Meek - Writer, poet, would-be singer, horticulturist, lyricist, strummer, wanderer, vegetarian, awkward guitarist.

Susan Broadfoot - Been writing on and off for years. Written half a dozen short stories for children, one soon to be a musical. Took to songwriting in my fifties and living it. Prefer doing lyrics but I have a go at tunes. Dabbled in music theatre, folk music, classical singing. Sing in an Abba tribute band and as guest with several other bands. Got a few recording projects on the go. Recently collaborated on a project with Uri Geller.

Bobbie O'neill (Aged 8 ¼) - Grandson of Andy Greenhouse.

George Colkitto - Winner of the Scottish Writers Poetry Competition 2012, Siar Sceal Hanna Greally Poetry Award 2014, Autumn Voices acrostic competition 2020, has poems in Linwood, Johnstone, and Erskine Health Centres. Recent publications are two poetry collections from Diehard Press and a pamphlet from Cinnamon Press.

Janette Fenton - Was born in Glasgow, raised in The Highlands and lives in London. She is a semi-retired teacher who is also a singer songwriter, poet and environmentalist, who has a passion for words and music and the planet. Janette has released three songs on Amazon, bandcamp, Apple, Spotify etc: Face Me, Ghost of Life and That's How Close. That's How Close has been played on American iheart radio and on BBC Radio. It has also been entered for a Now That's What I call Lockdown compilation, which will go into the British Museum lockdown archives. Janette enjoys writing with others and has co-written the song So Easy by Steve Kopandy. She also runs the iconic music venue Facebook group, the Marquee Club, London.

Andy Greenhouse - Was born in London on 23rd October 1956. He is a poet, a folksinger and a songwriter. As a child he heard hymns in church, his mother singing Palgrave's Golden Treasury and the Beatles. Later it was Kerouac, Shakespeare and the Marx Brothers, now it is Yeats, Burnside and Heaney. Nothing much changes. He has self-published 3 volumes of poetry, released a dozen albums and is host of the Invisible Folk Club radio show and podcast.

George Bakolas - Is a director-playwright-scriptwriter based in Berlin. He is a graduate of the Stavrakos Film School in Athens. His plays, directed both by himself and others, have been staged in Greece and abroad (England, Ireland, Germany). He has directed four experimental feature films and published two collections of novels. He has participated in several international festivals and has been awarded for his movies and scripts.

Jon Bickley - Was born in London on 23rd October 1956. He is a poet, a folksinger and a songwriter. As a child he heard hymns in church, his mother singing Palgrave's Golden Treasury and the Beatles. Later it was Kerouac, Shakespeare and the Marx Brothers, now it is Yeats, Burnside and Heaney. Nothing much changes. He has self-published 3 volumes of poetry, released a dozen albums and is host of the Invisible Folk Club radio show and podcast.

Mark Ingram - Is committed to positive social change a supporter of CND and Green issues. A dedicated union officer protecting workers rights is a main driving force in his life. He lives in Lichfield with his partner Carol and Maxwell the cat and enjoys walking, reading and writing poetry and prose.

Acknowledgements -

A massive debt of gratitude to all contributors, past and present. None of this, and what we do, would take place without your unstinting support.

And to you the reader.

Keep on writing!

Meek

November

2022.

Publisher

INHERIT THE EARTH PUBLICATIONS.

ONLINE PUBLISHERS.

inherit_theearth@btinternet.com

Notes.